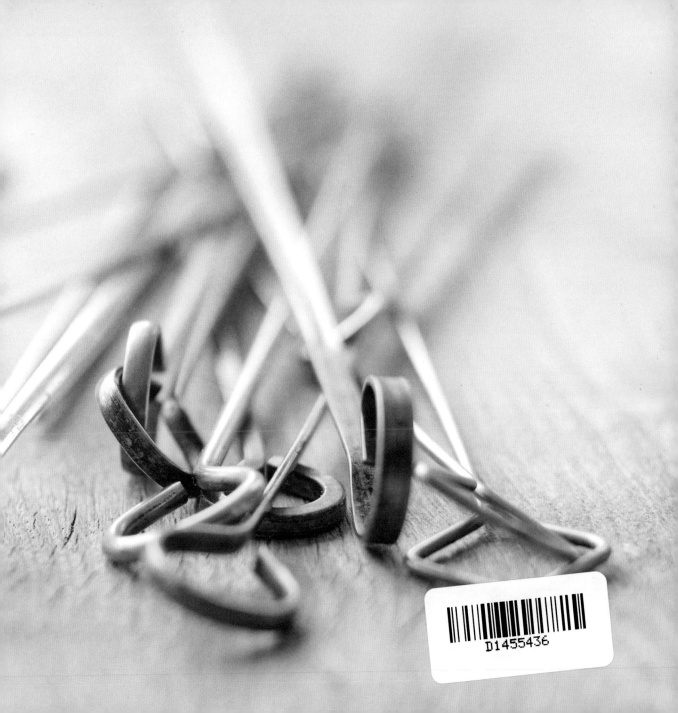

kabobs
& other light grills

kabobs
& other light grills

Ghillie Başan

photography by Richard Jung

RYLAND
PETERS
& SMALL

LONDON NEW YORK

Dedication
For Nina. Even you can cook with this book!

Senior Designer Sonya Nathoo
Senior Commissioning Editor Julia Charles
Photographic Art Direction Megan Smith
Production Controller Toby Marshall
Art Director Leslie Harrington
Publishing Director Alison Starling

Prop Stylist Róisín Nield
Food Stylist Sunil Vijayaker
Indexer Hilary Bird

First published in 2010 by Ryland Peters & Small, Inc.
519 Broadway, 5th Floor
New York, NY 10012
www.rylandpeters.com

10 9 8 7 6 5 4 3 2

Text © Ghillie Başan 2010
Design and photographs © Ryland Peters & Small 2010

Printed and bound in China

Library of Congress Cataloging-in-Publication Data
Basan, Ghillie.
  Kabobs and other light grills / Ghillie Basan ; photography by Richard Jung.
    p. cm.
  Includes index.
  ISBN 978-1-84597-974-4
  1. Skewer cookery. 2. Barbecue cookery. I. Title.
  TX834.B384 2010
  641.7'6--dc22
                                    2009046603

Author's acknowledgments
As always, I have many people to thank on my travels, but the book itself would never have come about without the support of my editor, Julia Charles, who is always a delight to work with. My thanks also go to Richard, Megan, Sonya, Ròisìn, and Sunil, for making this book look so appetizing.

Contents

Introduction   6

Meat   8

Poultry   22

Fish   34

Vegetables   48

Accompaniments   58

Index   64

Introduction

The story of the kabob and its Southeast Asian cousin, the satay, is really a very old one as it can be traced back to the early travelers, hunters, and nomadic peoples who would set up fires to ward off wild animals and provide warmth as well as to roast a whole beast, but the invention of skewering small cuts of meat onto sticks and metal swords is much more recent and its origins can be attributed to the Persians and Arabs of the Middle Ages. Now known universally as the "kabob" or "kebab", this traditional method spread with Islamic Empire across the Middle East, North Africa, India, and Pakistan and later made an impact on the cultures of Indo-China where the method became known as "satay."

Originally, kabobs were invented as a way of using up poor cuts of meat, often marinated with spices to tenderize and disguise any flaws, but the method rendered the meat so tasty that kabob houses and satay stalls became features of their respective culinary landscape. In the Middle East and North Africa the kabob is generally the main part of a meal and therefore may be served on its own with lemon to squeeze over it, whereas the satay dishes of Southeast Asia are often served as snacks or as part of a banquet and are invariably accompanied by a fiery relish or a dipping sauce.

The key to all kabobs is the marinating and basting to render the meat or fish tender, tasty, and juicy. Skewers are also an important feature. Most meat kabobs are cooked and served on metal skewers, which retain a higher heat and cook the inside of the meat; vegetable and fish kabobs are often cooked on wooden skewers, some of which can enhance the flavor, such as cherry, juniper, and birch; and satay dishes are often prepared on wooden or bamboo skewers, which need to be soaked in water before use, although some local specialities thread the ingredients onto stalks of sugar cane or lemongrass for flavor and effect. Light and delicious, cooked on a charcoal grill or under a hot broiler, kabobs are simple and versatile food for any time of the year.

meat

For the kabobs:

1 lb. finely ground lean lamb

1 onion, grated

2 teaspoons ground cumin

1 teaspoon ground coriander

1 teaspoon paprika

½–1 teaspoon cayenne pepper

1 teaspoon sea salt

a small bunch of fresh flat-leaf parsley, finely chopped

a small bunch of cilantro, finely chopped

For the hot hummus:

1½ cups dried chickpeas, soaked overnight and cooked in plenty of water until tender, or a 14-oz. can cooked chickpeas, drained

3 tablespoons olive oil

freshly squeezed juice of 1 lemon

1 teaspoon cumin seeds

2 tablespoons light tahini

4 tablespoons thick, strained plain yogurt

sea salt and freshly ground black pepper

2½ tablespoons butter

To serve:

leafy salad greens

flatbreads

2 metal skewers with wide, flat blades

Serves 4–6

Cumin-flavored lamb kebabs with hot hummus

Typical fodder at the street grills or kabob houses, these kabobs are enjoyed throughout the Middle East and North Africa. To prepare them successfully, you will need large metal skewers with wide, flat blades to hold the meat, which acts like a sheath to the sword.

Mix the ground lamb with the other ingredients and knead well. Pound the meat to a smooth consistency in a large mortar and pestle, or whizz in a food processor. Leave to sit for an hour to let the flavors mingle.

Meanwhile, make the hummus. Preheat the oven to 400°F. In a food processor, whizz the chickpeas with the olive oil, lemon juice, cumin seeds, tahini, and yogurt. Season to taste, tip the mixture into an ovenproof dish, cover with foil, and put in the preheated oven to warm through.

Wet your hands to make the meat mixture easier to handle. Mold portions of the mixture around the skewers, squeezing and flattening it, so it looks like the sheath to the sword.

Prepare a charcoal grill or heat the broiler. Cook the kabobs for 4–5 minutes on each side. Quickly melt the butter and pour it over the hummus. When the kabobs are cooked on both sides, slip the meat off the skewers, cut into bite-size pieces and serve with the hot hummus on the side with leafy salad greens and flatbreads.

For the kabob:

1 lb. lean ground lamb

2 onions, finely chopped

1 fresh green chile, finely chopped

4 garlic cloves, crushed

1 teaspoon paprika

1 teaspoon ground sumac
(see note on page 38)

leaves from a small bunch of fresh
flat-leaf parsley, finely chopped

For the sauce:

2 tablespoons olive oil plus
a nut of butter

1 onion, finely chopped

2 garlic cloves, finely chopped

1 fresh green chile, seeded
and finely chopped

1 teaspoon sugar

14-oz. can chopped tomatoes

sea salt and freshly ground
black pepper

To serve:

2 tablespoons butter

8 plum tomatoes

1 large pide or plain naan bread,
cut into pieces

1 teaspoon ground sumac

1 teaspoon dried oregano

1 cup thick plain yogurt

a bunch of fresh flat-leaf parsley,
chopped

*1 large metal skewer with a wide,
flat blade, plus 1 long thin skewer*

Serves 4

Lamb shish kabob
with yogurt and flatbread

To my mind this is the ultimate kabob! There are variations throughout the Middle East but this tasty Turkish version, designed to use up day-old "pide" bread, is outstanding.

Put the ground lamb in a bowl. Add all the other kabob ingredients and knead well, until it resembles a smooth paste and is quite sticky. Cover and chill in the refrigerator for about 15 minutes.

To make the sauce, heat the oil and butter in a heavy-based saucepan. Add the onion, garlic, and chile, and stir until they begin to color. Add the sugar and tomatoes and cook, uncovered, until quite thick and saucey. Season to taste. Keep warm.

Wet your hands to make the meat mixture easier to handle. Mold portions of the mixture around the skewer, squeezing and flattening it, so it looks like the sheath to the sword. Thread the tomatoes onto the thin skewer.

Prepare a charcoal grill or heat the broiler. Cook the kabob for 4–5 minutes on each side. Add the tomatoes to the grill and cook until charred and soft. While both are cooking, melt the butter in a heavy-based skillet, add the pide pieces and toss until golden. Sprinkle with some of the sumac and oregano and arrange on a serving plate. Spoon some sauce and half the yogurt on top.

When the kabob is cooked on both sides, slip the meat off the skewer, cut into large pieces and arrange on top of the pide along with the tomatoes. Sprinkle with salt and the remaining sumac and oregano. Add the sauce and yogurt and garnish with parsley.

For the satay:

1 lb. pork tenderloin, cut into bite-size cubes or strips

For the marinade:

4 shallots, peeled and chopped

4 garlic cloves, peeled

2–3 teaspoons Indian curry powder

2 tablespoons dark soy sauce

2 tablespoons sesame or peanut oil

For the pineapple sauce:

4 shallots, peeled and chopped

2 garlic cloves, chopped

4 dried red chiles, soaked in warm water until soft, seeded, and chopped

1 lemongrass stalk, trimmed and chopped

1-inch piece of fresh ginger, peeled and chopped

2 tablespoons sesame or peanut oil

¾ cup coconut milk

2 teaspoons tamarind paste (see note on page 37)

2 teaspoons sugar

1 small fresh pineapple, peeled, cored, and cut into slices

sea salt

To serve:

Rice Pilaf (see page 61), optional

a package of short wooden or bamboo skewers, soaked in water before use

Serves 4

Curried pork satay with pineapple sauce

This spicy satay is popular in Malaysia and Singapore. A combination of Indian, Malay, and Chinese traditions, it is best accompanied by a rice pilaf or chunks of bread.

To make the marinade, use a mortar and pestle, or a food processor, to pound the shallots and garlic to form a paste. Stir in the curry powder and soy sauce, and bind with the oil. Rub the marinade into the meat, making sure it is well coated. Cover and refrigerate for at least 2 hours.

In the meantime, prepare the sauce. Using a mortar and pestle, or a food processor, pound the shallots, garlic, chiles, lemongrass, and ginger to form a paste. Heat the oil in a heavy-based pan and stir in the paste. Cook for 2–3 minutes until fragrant and beginning to color, then stir in the coconut milk, tamarind, and sugar. Bring the mixture to a boil, then reduce the heat and simmer for about 5 minutes. Season to taste and let cool. Using a mortar and pestle, or a food processor, crush 3 slices of the fresh pineapple and beat them into the sauce.

Prepare a charcoal grill or heat the broiler. Thread the marinated meat onto the prepared skewers. Line them up over the hot charcoal or on the broiler pan and place the remaining slices of pineapple beside them. Char the pineapple slices and chop them into chunks. Grill the meat until just cooked, roughly 2–3 minutes each side, and serve immediately with the charred pineapple chunks for spearing, and the sauce for dipping.

For the satay:

1 lb. beef sirloin, cut against the grain into bite-size pieces

1 tablespoon peanut oil

For the peanut sauce:

¼ cup peanut or vegetable oil

4–5 garlic cloves, crushed

4–5 dried serrano chiles, seeded and ground in a pestle and mortar

1–2 teaspoons curry powder

½ cup roasted peanuts, finely ground

To serve:

a small bunch of cilantro

a small bunch of fresh mint

lime wedges

a package of short wooden or bamboos skewers, soaked in water before use

Serves 4–6

Fiery beef satay in peanut sauce

Beef, pork, or chicken satays cooked in, or served with, a fiery peanut sauce are popular throughout Southeast Asia. This particular sauce is a great favorite in Thailand, Vietnam, and Indonesia. It is best to make your own but commercial brands are available under the banner satay or sate sauce.

To make the sauce, heat the oil in a heavy-based saucepan and stir in the garlic until it begins to color. Add the chiles, curry powder, and the peanuts and stir over a gentle heat, until the mixture forms a paste. Remove from the heat and leave to cool.

Put the beef pieces in a bowl. Beat the peanut oil into the sauce and tip the mixture onto the beef. Mix well, so that the beef is evenly coated and thread the meat onto the prepared skewers.

Prepare a charcoal grill or heat the broiler. Cook the satays for 2–3 minutes on each side, then serve the skewered meat with the refreshing herbs to wrap around each tasty morsel.

For the sweet and sour sauce:

2 teaspoons peanut oil

1 garlic clove, finely chopped

1 fresh red chile, seeded and
finely chopped

2 tablespoons roasted peanuts,
finely chopped

1 tablespoon Thai fish sauce

2 tablespoons rice wine vinegar

2 tablespoons hoisin sauce

4 tablespoons coconut milk

1–2 teaspoons sugar, to taste

a pinch of sea salt

For the kofta (meatballs):

2 teaspoons peanut or sesame oil

4 shallots, finely chopped

2 garlic cloves, finely chopped

1 lb. ground pork

2 tablespoons Thai fish sauce

2 teaspoons five-spice powder

2 teaspoons sugar

2 handfuls of fresh white or
brown bread crumbs

sea salt and freshly ground
black pepper

To serve:

Simple Noodles (see page 61)

a small bunch of cilantro

*a package of wooden or
bamboo skewers, soaked
in water before use*

Serves 4

Pork kofta kabobs
with sweet and sour sauce

These Asian-style meatball kabobs are best served with
a hot, spicy dipping sauce and noodles. The sweet hoisin
sauce is available in larger supermarkets and Asian markets.

To make the sauce, heat the oil in a small wok or heavy-based skillet.
Stir in the garlic and chile and, when they begin to color, add the
peanuts. Stir for a few minutes until the natural oil from the peanuts
begins to weep. Add all the remaining ingredients (except the sugar
and salt) along with ½ cup water. Let the mixture bubble up for
1 minute. Adjust the sweetness and seasoning to taste with sugar
and some salt and set aside.

To make the meatballs, heat the oil in a wok or a heavy-based skillet.
Add the shallots and garlic—when they begin to brown, turn off the
heat and leave to cool. Put the ground pork into a bowl, tip in the
stir-fried shallot and garlic, fish sauce, five-spice powder, and sugar and
season with a little salt and lots of pepper. Using your hands, knead
the mixture so it is well combined. Cover and chill in the refrigerator
for 2–3 hours. Knead the mixture again then tip in the bread crumbs.
Knead well to bind. Divide the mixture into roughly 20 portions and
roll into balls. Thread them onto the prepared skewers. Prepare
a charcoal grill or heat the broiler. Cook the kebabs for 3–4 minutes
on each side, turning them from time to time, until browned.

Reheat the sauce. Serve the kofta with noodles and the hot sweet
and sour sauce on the side for dipping.

Spicy beef and coconut kofta kabobs

For the kofta (meatballs):

1 teaspoon coriander seeds

1 teaspoon cumin seeds

1⅓ cups desiccated or freshly grated coconut

1 tablespoon coconut oil

4 shallots, peeled and finely chopped

2 garlic cloves, finely chopped

1–2 fresh red chiles, seeded and finely chopped

12 oz. lean ground beef

1 beaten egg, to bind

sea salt and freshly ground black pepper

To serve:

2–3 tablespoons freshly grated or desiccated coconut

lime wedges

a package of short wooden or bamboo skewers, soaked in water before use

Serves 4

Variations of this Asian dish can be found at street stalls from Sri Lanka to the Philippines and South Africa to the West Indies. Simple and tasty, the kofta are delicious served with wedges of fresh lime or a dipping sauce of your choice.

In a small heavy-based skillet, dry roast the coriander and cumin seeds until they give off a nutty aroma. Using a mortar and pestle, or a spice grinder, grind the roasted seeds to a powder.

In the same pan, dry roast the coconut until it begins to color and give off a nutty aroma. Tip it onto a plate to cool.

Heat the coconut oil in the same small heavy-based pan and stir in the shallots, garlic, and chiles, until fragrant and beginning to color. Tip them onto a plate to cool.

Put the ground beef in a bowl and add the ground spices, toasted coconut, and shallot mixture. Season with salt and pepper and use a fork to mix all the ingredients together, adding a little egg to bind it (you may not need it all.) Knead the mixture with your hands and mold it into little balls. Thread the balls onto the prepared skewers.

Prepare a charcoal grill or heat the broiler. Cook the kabobs for 2–3 minutes on each side. Sprinkle the cooked kofta with the toasted coconut and serve with the wedges of lime to squeeze over them.

Lamb and porcini kabobs with sage and parmesan

1 lb. tender lamb, from the leg or shoulder, cut into bite-size pieces

4–8 fresh medium-sized porcini, cut into quarters or thickly sliced

2 tablespoons olive oil

freshly squeezed juice of 1–2 lemons

leaves from a bunch of fresh sage, finely chopped (reserve a few whole leaves)

2 garlic cloves, crushed

sea salt and freshly ground black pepper

To serve:

truffle oil, to drizzle

Parmesan shavings

grilled or toasted sourdough bread

4 long, thin metal skewers

Serves 4

Rural feasts in Italy often involve grilling outdoors. One of the most exciting times is the mushroom season when entire villages hunt for wild mushrooms and gather together to cook them. These kabobs are prepared with freshly picked porcini, but you could substitute them with other meaty wild or cremini mushrooms or dried porcini reconstituted in water.

Put the lamb pieces in a bowl and toss in half the oil and lemon juice. Add the sage and garlic and season with salt and pepper. Cover, refrigerate, and leave to marinate for about 2 hours.

Thread the lamb onto skewers adding a quarter, or slice, of porcini every so often with a sage leaf. Brush with any of the marinade left in the bowl. Prepare a charcoal grill or heat the broiler. Cook the kabobs for 3–4 minutes on each side.

Serve immediately with a drizzle of truffle oil and Parmesan shavings and toasted sourdough bread, if liked.

Harissa chicken kabobs
with oranges and preserved lemon

16–20 chicken wings

4 oranges (blood oranges if available), cut into quarters

¼ cup confectioners' sugar

½ a preserved lemon*, finely shredded or chopped

a small bunch of cilantro, chopped

For the marinade:

4 tablespoons harissa paste (see note on page 54)

2 tablespoons olive oil

sea salt

4 long, thin metal skewers

Serves 4

With a taste of North Africa, this recipe is quick and easy and best eaten with fingers. The oranges are there to suck on after an explosion of fire on the tongue. They can be cooked separately, or threaded alternately on metal skewers.

Mix the harissa with the olive oil to form a looser paste and add a little salt. Brush the oily mixture over the chicken wings, so that they're well coated. Leave to marinate for 2 hours.

Thread the marinated chicken wings onto the skewers. Prepare a charcoal grill or heat the broiler. Cook on both sides for about 5 minutes. Once the wings begin to cook, dip the orange quarters lightly in confectioners' sugar, thread them onto skewers and grill them for a few minutes, checking that they are slightly charred but not burnt.

Serve the chicken wings and oranges together and scatter the preserved lemon and cilantro over the top.

*Note Preserved lemons are used extensively in North African cooking and are whole lemons packed in jars with salt. The interesting thing is that you eat only the peel, which contains the essential flavor of the lemon. They are available from supermarkets and online retailers.

Lemon chicken kabobs
wrapped in eggplant

freshly squeezed juice of
2–3 lemons

2 garlic cloves, crushed

4–6 allspice berries, crushed

1 tablespoon crushed dried
sage leaves

8 chicken thighs, boned
and skinned

4 eggplants

safflower oil, for deep-frying

1 tablespoon butter

To serve:

lemon wedges, to serve

salad of your choice

Rice Pilaf (see page 61)

*4 metal or wooden skewers,
to serve (optional)*

an ovenproof dish, well greased

Serves 4

This Ottoman dish is impressive and tasty and best served
with a refreshing salad, such as tomato and cucumber, or
parsley, pepper, and onion, and a buttery rice pilaf.

Preheat the oven to 350°F.

In a shallow bowl, mix together the lemon juice, garlic, allspice berries,
and sage leaves. Toss the chicken thighs in the mixture, rolling them
over in the juice, and let marinate for about 2 hours.

Peel the eggplants in strips and slice them thinly lengthwise, so that
you have at least 16 long strips. Soak the strips in a bowl of cold, salted
water for about 30 minutes. Drain and squeeze out the excess water.
In a wok or large skillet, heat sufficient oil for deep-frying and fry the
eggplants in batches, until golden brown. Drain on paper towels.

On a board or plate, lay two eggplant strips, one over the other in
a cross, then place a marinated chicken thigh in the middle. Pull
the eggplant strips over the thigh to form a neat package. Place the
package, seam-side down, in the prepared ovenproof dish and repeat
the process with the remaining thighs. Pour the rest of the marinade
over the top and dab each parcel with butter. Cover the dish with foil
and cook in the preheated oven for 30 minutes. Remove the foil, baste
the chicken parcels with the cooking juices, and return to the oven for
a further 10 minutes. Serve immediately, threaded onto skewers to
secure them (if using), with wedges of lemon on the side for squeezing
and a salad and rice pilaf.

2¼ lbs. chicken breasts, cut into bite-size pieces

2 tablespoons ghee or butter, melted

For the marinade:

3 fresh red or green chiles, seeded and chopped

2–3 garlic cloves, chopped

1 oz. fresh ginger, peeled and chopped

2 tablespoons heavy cream

3 tablespoons vegetable oil

1 tablespoon paprika

2 teaspoons ground cumin

2 teaspoons ground cardamom

1 teaspoon ground cloves

1 teaspoon sea salt

To serve (optional):

crispy poppadoms

tomato and cucumber salad

limes wedges

4–6 long, thin metal skewers

Serves 4–6

Chicken tandoori kabobs

As the name of this dish denotes, it should be cooked in a tandoori oven but, as most of us don't have such a wonderful invention at home, a charcoal grill is a good substitute. Some Indian and African cooks add red food dye to the marinade to obtain the reddish coloring associated with tandoori dishes.

To prepare the marinade, use a mortar and pestle, or an electric blender, to mince the chiles, garlic, and ginger to a paste. Beat in the cream and oil with 3–4 tablespoons water to form a smooth mixture. Beat in the dried spices.

Place the chicken pieces in a bowl and rub with the marinade until thoroughly coated. Cover and chill in the refrigerator for about 48 hours. Lift the chicken pieces out of the marinade and thread them onto the skewers. Prepare a charcoal grill or heat the broiler. Brush the chicken with the melted ghee and cook for 3–4 minutes. Serve with crispy poppadoms, a salad of finely diced tomato, cucumber, and onion with cilantro, and wedges of lime for squeezing, if liked.

2 lbs. chicken breasts, cut into
bite-size pieces

2 tablespoons ghee or butter,
melted

For the marinade:

1¾ cups thick plain yogurt,
left to drain through cheesecloth
for 1–2 hours

2 oz. fresh ginger, peeled and
pounded to a pulp

2–3 garlic cloves, crushed

2 teaspoons chili powder

2 teaspoons ground cinnamon

2 teaspoons ground cumin

1 teaspoon ground coriander

1 teaspoon ground cardamom

1 teaspoon ground cloves

1 teaspoon ground black pepper

1–2 teaspoons salt

freshly squeezed juice of 1 lemon

For the minted yogurt:

6 tablespoons thick plain yogurt

freshly squeezed juice of ½ a lemon

2 garlic cloves, crushed

sea salt and freshly ground
black pepper

leaves from a small bunch of fresh
mint, finely chopped or shredded

*a package of short wooden or
bamboo skewers, soaked in
water before use*

Serves 4–6

Gingery chicken tikka kabobs with minted yogurt

This version of the classic Indian tikka is incredibly versatile as you can vary the spices according to your taste and you can serve the tasty little bits of chicken with drinks, as a snack tucked into pitta bread, or as part of barbecue spread. It is delicious served with this refreshing minted yogurt or your favorite fruit chutney.

To prepare the marinade, beat together the strained yogurt, ginger, and garlic then stir in the spices and lemon juice. Toss the chicken pieces in the marinade, making sure they are thoroughly coated. Cover, refrigerate, and leave to marinate for at least 2 hours.

Meanwhile, prepare the minted yogurt. Beat the yogurt with the lemon juice and garlic. Season to taste and stir in the mint. Set aside.

Thread the chicken onto the prepared skewers, leaving behind any excess marinade, and brush the melted ghee over them. Prepare a charcoal grill or heat the broiler. Cook the kabobs for about 3 minutes on each side, until the chicken is nicely browned and cooked through. Serve with the minted yogurt on the side for dipping.

Spicy chicken kabobs
with ground almonds

1 lb. 9 oz. chicken breasts, cut into bite-size pieces

freshly squeezed juice of 1 lemon

1 teaspoon sea salt

1–2 tablespoons peanut or safflower oil

1 onion, halved and sliced

1 oz. fresh ginger, peeled and finely grated

2 garlic cloves, crushed

2–3 tablespoons ground almonds

1–2 teaspoons garam masala

½ cup heavy cream

To serve:

1–2 tablespoons butter

2–3 tablespoons blanched, slivered almonds

a small bunch of fresh flat-leaf parsley, finely chopped

warmed flatbreads

4 long, thin metal skewers

Serves 4

In India, Turkey, and North Africa, nuts are often used in recipes. Sometimes they are hidden in the ground meat of a kofta (meatball), or they form a coating on the meat. In this dish, the combination of ground almonds and browned onions in the marinade gives the meat a sweet, rich flavor.

First toss the chicken pieces in the lemon juice and salt to blanch them. Put aside for 15 minutes.

Meanwhile, heat the oil in a skillet. Add the onion and cook until golden brown and crisp. Remove the onion from the oil and spread it out on a sheet of paper towel to drain and cool. Reserve the oil in the skillet.

Using a mortar and pestle, or an electric blender, pound the onions to a paste and beat in the ginger and garlic. Add the almonds and garam masala and bind with the cream. Tip the almond and onion mixture over the chicken and mix well. Cover and leave in the refrigerator to marinate for about 6 hours.

Thread the chicken onto the skewers and brush them with the reserved onion oil. Prepare a charcoal grill or heat the broiler. Cook the kabobs for 3–4 minutes on each side, until the chicken is nicely browned. Quickly melt the butter in a pan and stir in the slivered almonds until golden. Toss in the parsley and spoon the mixture over the grilled chicken. Serve hot with warmed flatbreads, if liked.

Duck satay with grilled pineapple and plum sauce

1 lb. 9 oz. duck breasts or boned thighs, sliced into thin, bite-size strips

1–2 tablespoons peanut or coconut oil, for brushing

1 small pineapple, peeled, cored, and sliced

Chinese plum sauce, to serve

For the marinade:

2–3 tablespoons light soy sauce

freshly squeezed juice of 1 lime

1–2 teaspoons sugar

1–2 garlic cloves, crushed

1 oz. fresh ginger, peeled and finely grated

1 small onion, grated

1–2 teaspoons ground coriander

1 teaspoon salt

a package of wooden or bamboo skewers, soaked in water before use

Serves 4

Chicken satays are popular throughout Southeast Asia but in Vietnam, Cambodia, and China, duck satays are common too. Duck is often served in the Chinese tradition of sweet and sour with a fruity sauce. You can buy prepared bottled plum sauce in Chinese grocers and most supermarkets.

To make the marinade, put the soy sauce and lime juice in a bowl with the sugar and mix until it dissolves. Add the garlic, ginger, and grated onion and stir in the coriander and salt.

Place the strips of duck in a bowl and pour over the marinade. Toss well, cover, and chill in the refrigerator for at least 4 hours. Thread the duck strips onto the skewers and brush them with oil.

Prepare a charcoal grill or heat the broiler. Cook the satays for 3–4 minutes on each side, until the duck is nicely browned. Grill the slices of pineapple at the same time. When browned, cut them into bite-size pieces and serve with the duck. Drizzle with the plum sauce to serve.

about 30 preserved vine leaves

4–5 large, skinless fillets of white fish, with all bones removed

For the marinade:

2–3 garlic cloves, crushed

1–2 teaspoons ground cumin

4 tablespoons olive oil

freshly squeezed juice of 1 lemon

1 teaspoon sea salt

For the tangy herb sauce:

¼ cup white wine vinegar or freshly squeezed lemon juice

1–2 tablespoons sugar

a pinch of saffron threads

1 onion, finely chopped

2 garlic cloves, finely chopped

2–3 scallions, finely sliced

a thumb-size piece of fresh ginger, grated

2 fresh hot red or green chiles, finely sliced

a small bunch of cilantro, finely chopped

a small bunch of fresh mint, finely chopped

sea salt

a package of short wooden or bamboo skewers, soaked in water before use

Serves 4

Vine-wrapped fish kabobs with tangy herb sauce

For these Mediterranean kabobs, almost any kind of firm, white fish fillet will do—monkfish or haddock work well. The fish is prepared in a simple marinade and then wrapped in the vine leaves, which become crisper with cooking.

First wash the vine leaves and soak them in several changes of water for 1 hour.

To prepare the marinade, mix all the ingredients together in a shallow bowl. Cut each fillet of fish into roughly 8 bite-size pieces and coat in the marinade. Cover and chill in the refrigerator for 1 hour.

Meanwhile, prepare the tangy herb sauce. Put the vinegar in a small saucepan with the sugar and 1–2 tablespoons water. Heat until the sugar has dissolved. Bring to a boil for 1 minute, then leave to cool. Add the other ingredients, mix well and spoon it into small individual bowls.

Lay the prepared vine leaves on a flat surface and place a piece of marinated fish in the center of each one. Fold the edges over the fish and wrap the leaf up into a small package. Push the packages onto the individual skewers and brush with any remaining marinade.

Prepare a charcoal grill or heat the broiler. Cook the kabobs for 2–3 minutes on each side. Serve immediately with a dish of tangy herb sauce on the side for dipping.

fish

Char-grilled tamarind shrimp

1 lb. 2 oz. fresh, jumbo shrimp, deveined and trimmed of heads, feelers, and legs

For the marinade:

3 tablespoons tamarind pulp*

1 cup warm water

2 tablespoons sweet soy sauce

1 tablespoon sugar

freshly ground black pepper

To serve:

leaves from a small bunch of cilantro

2–4 fresh green chiles, seeded and sliced

a package of wooden or bamboo skewers, soaked in water before use

Serves 2–4

This is popular street food in Malaysia and Indonesia. The aroma emanating from the stalls as the marinated shrimp are grilled over charcoal, makes you feel very hungry.

Rinse the prepared shrimp well, pat dry and using a very sharp knife, make an incision along the curve of the tail. Set aside.

Put the tamarind pulp in a bowl and add the warm water. Soak the pulp, until soft, squeezing it with your fingers to help dissolve it. Strain the liquid and discard any fiber or seeds. In a bowl, mix together the tamarind juice, soy sauce, sugar, and black pepper. Pour it over the shrimp, rubbing it over the shells and into the incision in the tails. Cover, refrigerate, and leave to marinate for about 1 hour.

Insert a skewer into each marinated shrimp. Prepare a charcoal grill or heat the broiler. Cook the shrimp for about 3 minutes on each side, until the shrimp shells have turned orange, brushing them with the marinade as they cook. Serve immediately, garnished with the cilantro and chiles.

*Note Tamarind lends a rich, sweet-sour flavor to dishes. The tropical trees produce fresh pods that are either sold fresh or processed into pulp or paste for convenience and long shelf life. Look out for it in Asian or Caribbean grocers—semi-dried tamarind pulp comes in soft rectangular blocks sealed in plastic wrap. The darker concentrated paste is sold in tubs and is a more processed product.

1 lb. 2 oz. boned swordfish, cut
into bite-size chunks

2 oranges, cut into wedges

a handful of fresh bay leaves

2–3 teaspoons ground sumac*

For the marinade:

1 onion, grated

1–2 garlic cloves, crushed

freshly squeezed juice of ½ a lemon

2–3 tablespoons olive oil

1–2 teaspoons tomato paste

sea salt and freshly ground
black pepper

*4 metal skewers or 4 wooden
skewers, soaked in water
before use*

Serves 4

Swordfish kabobs
with oranges and sumac

Any firm-fleshed fish, such as tuna, trout, salmon, monkfish,
and sea bass, can be used for these mighty Middle Eastern
kabobs. Make life easy and buy the swordfish ready boned
from the fishmonger. Exotic sumac adds a lemony tang.

In a shallow bowl, mix together the ingredients for the marinade.
Toss the chunks of swordfish in the marinade, cover, and set aside
to marinate for 30 minutes.

Thread the marinated fish onto the skewers, alternating it with the
orange segments and the occasional bay leaf. If there is any marinade
left, brush it over the kabobs.

Prepare a charcoal grill or heat the broiler. Cook the kabobs for
2–3 minutes on each side, until the fish is nicely browned. Sprinkle
the kabobs with sumac and serve.

*Note Sumac is an increasingly popular spice. It grows wild, but
is also cultivated in Italy, Sicily, and throughout the Middle East. It is
widely used in Lebanese, Syrian, Turkish, and Iranian cooking. The
red berries have an astringent quality, with a pleasing sour-fruit flavor.
They are used whole, but ground sumac is available from Middle
Eastern grocers or specialist online retailers.

Monkfish kabobs with chermoula

2 lbs. monkfish tail, cut into chunks

12–16 cherry tomatoes

1–2 teaspoons smoked paprika

1–2 lemons, cut into wedges

For the chermoula:

2 garlic cloves

1 teaspoon coarse sea salt

1–2 teaspoons cumin seeds,
crushed or ground

1 fresh red chile, seeded
and chopped

freshly squeezed juice of 1 lemon

2 tablespoons olive oil

a small bunch of cilantro, roughly
chopped

*4–6 metal skewers or 4–6 wooden
skewers, soaked in water
before use*

Serves 4–6

Chermoula is a classic Moroccan flavoring of garlic, chile, cumin, and cilantro, which is employed as a marinade for fish and chicken tagines and grilled dishes. Any meaty, white fish can be used for this recipe but monkfish cooks particularly well over charcoal.

To make the chermoula, use a mortar and pestle to pound the garlic with the salt to a smooth paste. Add the cumin, chile, lemon juice, and olive oil and stir in the cilantro.

Place the fish chunks in a shallow dish and rub with the chermoula. Cover and chill in the refrigerator for 1–2 hours.

Thread the marinated monkfish and cherry tomatoes alternately onto the skewers. Prepare a charcoal grill or heat the broiler. Cook the kabobs for about 2 minutes on each side, until the monkfish is nicely browned. Dust with a little paprika and serve with wedges of lemon for squeezing over them.

Stuffed char-grilled sardines

4 good-sized fresh sardines

2 tablespoons olive oil

4–6 scallions, finely sliced

2–3 garlic cloves, crushed

1 teaspoon cumin seeds, crushed

1 teaspoon ground sumac
(see note on page 38)

1 tablespoon pine nuts

1 tablespoon currants, soaked
in warm water for 15 minutes
and drained

a small bunch of fresh flat-leaf
parsley finely chopped

sea salt and freshly ground
black pepper

For basting:

3 tablespoons olive oil

freshly squeezed juice of 1 lemon

1–2 teaspoons ground sumac

*4 wooden skewers, soaked in
water before use*

Serves 4

This dish is best made with good-sized plump, fresh sardines, which are slit from head to tail with the back bone removed. Full of mediterranean flavors, this is a great recipe for outdoor cooking on the barbecue while enjoying the summer sunshine.

To prepare the sardines, remove the bone, gently massage the area around it to loosen it. Using your fingers, carefully prise out the bone, snapping it off at each end, while keeping the fish intact. Rinse the fish and pat it dry before stuffing.

Heat the oil in a heavy-based pan and stir in the scallions until soft. Add the garlic, cumin, and sumac. Add the pine nuts and pre-soaked currants, and sauté until the pine nuts begin to turn golden. Toss in the parsley and season with salt and pepper. Leave to cool.

Place each sardine on a flat surface and spread the filling inside each one. Seal the fish by threading the skewers through the soft belly flaps.

Mix together the olive oil, lemon juice, and sumac and brush some of it over the sardines. Prepare a charcoal grill or heat the broiler. Cook the stuffed fish for 2–3 minutes on each side, basting them with the rest of the olive oil mixture. Serve immediately.

Peri-peri shrimp satay

24 jumbo shrimp, slit along the
back bone to remove the vein
and head

12 fresh lime or lemon leaves

For the peri-peri:

1½ sticks butter

3–4 garlic cloves, crushed

⅛ cup olive oil

4 dried red chiles, left whole

freshly squeezed juice of 2 lemons

sea salt

*4–6 wooden or bamboo skewers,
soaked in water before use*

Serves 4–6

Peri-peri is a chile- and lemon-flavored buttery oil used
for marinating chicken and fish and in East and West Africa.
A legacy of the Portuguese influence in the region, the oil
takes its name from the Portuguese word for bird's eye
chiles, peri-peri. This spicy satay makes a good appetizer.

To make the peri-peri, melt the butter in a skillet and stir in the garlic.
Set aside. Heat the olive oil in a separate pan and add the chiles. Turn
off the heat and leave the oil to cool with the chiles still in it. When
cool, transfer the oil to a mixing bowl and beat in the garlic-flavored
butter, lemon juice, and a little salt.

Thread the shrimp onto the prepared skewers, alternating them with
the lime or lemon leaves. Brush the shrimp with the peri-peri butter.
Prepare a charcoal grill or heat the broiler. Cook the satays for about
2 minutes on each side, basting them with the peri-peri, until the
shrimp shells have turned orange. Serve immediately with any
remaining peri-peri on the side for dipping.

Shrimp and scallop kabobs
with walnut sauce

12 jumbo shrimp, shelled
   to the tail

8 fresh scallops, shelled and
   thoroughly cleaned

8 cherry tomatoes

1 green bell pepper, cut into
   bite-size squares

For the marinade:

freshly squeezed juice of 2 lemons

4 garlic cloves, crushed

1 teaspoon ground cumin

1 teaspoon paprika

sea salt

For the walnut sauce:

1 cup shelled walnut halves

2 slices day-old bread, soaked
   in water and squeezed dry

2–3 garlic cloves, crushed

3–4 tablespoons olive oil

freshly squeezed juice of 1 lemon

a dash of white wine vinegar

sea salt and freshly ground
   black pepper

*4 wooden or bamboo skewers,
   soaked in water before use*

Serves 4

This is a popular way to enjoy the jumbo shrimp and scallops along the Mediterranean coast of Syria, Turkey, and Lebanon. Threaded onto skewers with bell peppers and tomatoes, they are served with a delicious garlicky walnut sauce.

To make the marinade, mix together the lemon juice, garlic, cumin, paprika, and a little salt in a bowl. Rub the mixture into the shrimp and scallops. Cover, refrigerate, and leave to marinate for about 1 hour.

Meanwhile, prepare the walnut sauce. Using a mortar and pestle, pound the walnuts to a paste, or whizz them in an electric blender. Add the bread and garlic and pound to a paste. Drizzle in the olive oil, stirring all the time, and beat in the lemon juice and vinegar. The sauce should be smooth with the consistency of heavy cream—if it's too dry, stir in a little water. Season with salt and pepper and set aside.

Thread the shrimp and scallops onto the skewers, alternating with the tomatoes and bell peppers, until all the ingredients are used up. Prepare a charcoal grill or heat the broiler. Cook the kabobs for 2 minutes on each side, basting with any of the leftover marinade, until the shrimp shells are orange, the scallops tender, and the tomatoes and bell peppers lightly browned. Serve hot with the walnut sauce on the side for dipping.

vegetables

Summer vegetable kabobs with homemade pesto sauce

2 eggplants, cut into chunks

2 zucchini, cut into chunks

2–3 bell peppers, stalks removed, seeded, and cut into chunks

12–16 cherry tomatoes

4 red onions, cut into quarters

For the marinade:

4 tablespoons olive oil

freshly squeezed juice of ½ a lemon

2 garlic cloves, crushed

1 teaspoon sea salt

For the pesto sauce:

3–4 garlic cloves, roughly chopped

leaves from a large bunch of fresh basil (at least 30–40 leaves)

½ teaspoon sea salt

2–3 tablespoons pine nuts

extra virgin olive oil, as required

¼ cup freshly grated Parmesan

4–6 metal skewers or 4–6 wooden skewers, soaked in water before use

Serves 4–6

Full of sunshine flavors, these kabobs can be served with couscous and a salad, or with pasta tossed in some of the pesto sauce. Homemade pesto is very personal—some people like it very garlicky, others prefer lots of basil or Parmesan—so simply adjust the quantities to suit your taste.

To make the pesto sauce, use a mortar and pestle to pound the garlic with the basil leaves and salt—the salt will act as an abrasive and help to grind. (If you only have small mortar and pestle, you may have to do this in batches.) Add the pine nuts and pound them to a paste. Slowly drizzle in some olive oil and bind with the grated Parmesan. Continue to pound and grind with the pestle, adding in enough oil to make a smooth sauce. Set aside.

Put all the prepared vegetables in a bowl. Mix together the olive oil, lemon juice, garlic, and salt and pour it over the vegetables. Using your hands, toss the vegetables gently in the marinade, then thread them onto the skewers.

Prepare a charcoal grill or heat the broiler. Cook the kabobs for 2–3 minutes on each side, until the vegetables are nicely browned. Serve the kabobs with the pesto sauce on the side for drizzling.

Spicy tofu satay
with soy dipping sauce

10 oz. firm tofu, rinsed, drained, patted dry, and cut into bite-size cubes

leaves from a small bunch of fresh basil, shredded, to serve

sesame oil, for frying

For the marinade:

3 lemongrass stalks, trimmed and finely chopped

1 tablespoon peanut oil

3 tablespoons soy sauce

1–2 fresh red chiles, seeded and finely chopped

2 garlic cloves, crushed

1 teaspoon ground turmeric

2 teaspoons sugar

sea salt

For the soy dipping sauce:

4–5 tablespoons soy sauce

1–2 tablespoons Thai fish sauce

freshly squeezed juice of 1 lime

1–2 teaspoons sugar

1 fresh red chile, seeded and finely chopped

3–4 wooden or bamboo skewers, soaked in water before use

Serves 3–4

Here is a very tasty dish that does wonderful things to tofu, which can be rather bland. Full of the flavors of Southeast Asia, this Vietnamese dish is sold at street stalls as a snack but serve it as an appetizer or with noodles as an entrée.

To make the marinade, mix the lemongrass, peanut oil, soy sauce, chile, garlic, and turmeric with the sugar until it has dissolved. Add a little salt to taste and toss in the tofu, making sure it is well coated. Leave to marinate for 1 hour.

Prepare the soy dipping sauce by whisking all the ingredients together. Set aside until ready to serve.

To cook the tofu, you can stir-fry the cubes in a wok with a little sesame oil and then thread them onto sticks to serve, or you can skewer them and grill them over charcoal or under the broiler for 2–3 minutes on each side. Serve the tofu hot, garnished with the shredded basil and with the soy dipping sauce on the side.

Roasted pumpkin wedges
with lime and spices

1 medium-size pumpkin, halved
   lengthwise, seeded, and cut
   into 6–8 segments

2 teaspoons coriander seeds

1 teaspoon cumin seeds

1 teaspoon fennel seeds

1–2 teaspoons ground cinnamon

2 dried red chiles, chopped

2 garlic cloves

2 tablespoons olive oil

coarse sea salt

finely grated peel of 1 lime

6 wooden or metal skewers,
   to serve (optional)

Serves 6

This is a great way to enjoy pumpkin. Serve these spicy wedges on their own or with any grilled, roasted, or barbecued meat or poultry dish. Save the seeds, roast them lightly with a little oil and coarse salt and enjoy as a snack.

Preheat the oven to 400°F.

Using a mortar and pestle, grind all the dried spices with the salt. Add the garlic and a little of the olive oil to form a paste. Rub the mixture over the pumpkin wedges and place them, skin-side down, in a baking dish or roasting pan. Cook them in the preheated oven for 35–40 minutes, or until tender. Sprinkle over the grated lime peel and serve hot, threaded onto skewers, if using.

Pan-grilled eggplant with honey and spices

8 eggplants, thickly sliced lengthwise

olive oil, for brushing

2–3 cloves garlic, crushed

a thumb-size piece of fresh ginger, peeled and crushed

1 teaspoon ground cumin

1 teaspoon harissa paste*

5 tablespoons runny honey

freshly squeezed juice of 1 lemon

sea salt

a small bunch of fresh flat-leaf parsley, finely chopped

Buttery Couscous (see page 58), to serve

4 metal or wooden skewers, to serve (optional)

Serves 4

Hot, spicy, sweet, and fruity are classic combinations of Moroccan cooking. In this delicious dish, these combinations send you on a thrilling journey. You can cook the eggplants in a ridged stovetop grill pan or under the broiler.

Brush each eggplant slice with olive oil and cook them in a stovetop grill pan or under the broiler, turning them over a few times so that they are lightly browned.

In a wok or large heavy skillet, fry the garlic in a little olive oil, then stir in the ginger, cumin, harissa, honey, and lemon juice. Add a little water to thin it, then place the eggplant slices in the liquid and cook gently for about 10 minutes, until they have absorbed the sauce. Add more water if necessary and season to taste with salt.

Thread the eggplant onto the skewers, if using, and garnish with the parsley. Serve hot or at room temperature as meal on their own with couscous, or as an accompaniment to grilled meat.

*Note Harissa is a fiercely hot red chile paste from North Africa, where it is used extensively as a condiment and diluted with stock, water, or fresh tomato sauce to flavor couscous dishes, soups, and tagines (stews.) Moroccan food is growing in popularity so harissa paste is now widely available in larger supermarkets and from specialist on-line retailers.

12 oz. cauliflower florets

safflower oil, for deep-frying

lime wedges, to serve

For the chutney:

1 onion, peeled and chopped

1–2 garlic cloves, peeled and chopped

leaves from a large bunch of cilantro

2–3 tablespoons freshly grated or desiccated coconut

1 teaspoon sugar

freshly squeezed juice of ½ a lemon

sea salt

For the batter:

1 cup plus 2 tablespoons gram (chickpea) flour

2 teaspoons ground turmeric

1 teaspoon ground coriander

1 teaspoon ground fenugreek

1 teaspoon cayenne pepper or chili powder

½ teaspoon baking soda

1–2 teaspoons cumin seeds, crushed

sea salt and freshly ground black pepper

a package of short wooden or bamboo skewers, to serve (optional)

Serves 4

Cauliflower fritter satay with cilantro and coconut chutney

Indian in style, these cauliflower fritters are served as a satay snack with a local chutney, Indonesian sweet soy sauce, or even tomato ketchup.

First prepare the cilantro and coconut chutney. Using a pestle and mortar, or an electric blender, pound the onion with the garlic and salt. Add the cilantro and pound to a paste. Beat in the coconut, sugar, and lemon juice and thin with a little water to form a smooth paste. Set aside.

Sift the gram flour with the ground spices and baking soda into a bowl. Add the cumin seeds and seasoning and bind with enough water to form a thick batter.

Heat sufficient oil in a wok or large skillet for deep-frying. Dip the cauliflower florets into the batter and drop them into the oil, working in batches, and cook until golden brown. Drain them on paper towels. Spear each cauliflower fritter with a skewer, if using, and serve hot with the cilantro and coconut chutney on the side for dipping.

Buttery couscous

2 cups couscous, rinsed and drained

1⅔ cups warm water plus ½ teaspoon sea salt

2 tablespoons safflower or olive oil

2 tablespoons butter, cut into small pieces

Serves 4–6

This is just a basic recipe to which you can add fresh herbs, a spice paste, or nuts and dried fruits of your choice.

Preheat the oven to 350°F.

Tip the couscous into an ovenproof dish. Pour the salted water over the couscous. Leave it to absorb the water for about 10 minutes. Using your fingers, rub the oil into the grains to break up the lumps and aerate them.

Scatter the butter over the surface and cover with a piece of foil or wet parchment paper. Put in the preheated oven for 15 minutes to heat through. Fluff up the grains with a fork before serving.

Bulgur with ghee

2 tablespoons ghee or 1 tablespoon olive oil plus a nut of butter

2 onions, chopped

2 cups bulgur (cracked wheat), thoroughly rinsed and drained

2½ cups vegetable or chicken stock or water

sea salt and freshly ground black pepper

Serves 4–6

Bulgur is delicious served with kabobs. You could add diced carrots, peas, spices, nuts, or herbs to this basic recipe.

Melt the ghee in a heavy-based saucepan. Add the onions and stir until soft. Add the bulgur, tossing it thoroughly with the onions.

Pour in the stock, season, and stir well. Bring to a boil and cook for 1–2 minutes, then reduce the heat and simmer, uncovered, until all the liquid has been absorbed. Turn off the heat, cover the pan with a clean kitchen towel, and press a lid on top. Leave to steam for a further 10–15 minutes, then fluff up with a fork before serving.

accompaniments

Rice pilaf

2¼ cups long grain rice, rinsed and soaked in water for 30 minutes

1–2 tablespoons ghee or 1 tablespoon olive oil plus a nut of butter

1 onion, chopped

1 teaspoon sugar

4–6 cardamom pods, bashed to release flavor from the seeds

4 cloves

2⅓ cups water plus 1 teaspoon sea salt

Serves 4–6

This recipe is the base to which other ingredients, such as nuts, ginger, and coconut, can be added. Ground turmeric and saffron can also be added for fragrance and color.

Heat the ghee in a heavy-based saucepan. Add the onion and sugar and fry until golden. Add the cardamom pods and cloves and stir in the pre-soaked rice, making sure the grains are coated in the ghee. Pour the salted water over the rice and bring to a boil.

Reduce the heat and simmer for 15–20 minutes, uncovered, until the liquid has been absorbed. Turn off the heat, cover the saucepan with a clean kitchen towel, followed by a lid, and leave the rice to steam for a further 10 minutes before fluffing up and serving.

Simple noodles with ginger and chile

8 oz. dried rice, wheat, or egg noodles

1–2 tablespoons vegetable oil

1 oz. fresh ginger, peeled and shredded

1–2 fresh red chiles, seeded, and finely chopped

1–2 garlic cloves, finely chopped

3–4 tablespoons soy sauce

2–3 teaspoons runny honey

leaves from a small bunch of cilantro, finely chopped

Serves 4

These simple noodles are good served with satay dishes and can also form the base of a more creative dish with shredded cabbage, julienned carrot, beansprouts, tofu, and peanuts.

Soak the noodles in water according to the package instructions. Heat the oil in a wok or large skillet. Add the ginger, chiles, and garlic and stir-fry until fragrant and just beginning to color. Toss in the reconstituted noodles and add the soy sauce and honey. Stir well. Toss in the chopped cilantro and serve immediately.

Roasted sweet potato
with garlic and ginger

2–3 good-size sweet potatoes,
  peeled and cut into chunks

a thumb-size piece of fresh ginger,
  peeled and cut into thin strips

4–6 garlic cloves, smashed

3–4 tablespoons olive oil

sea salt and freshly ground
  black pepper

To serve (optional):

lemon wedges

thick plain yogurt

Serves 4

Sweet potato is delicious roasted as the natural sugars caramelize in the oil and the softened flesh absorbs the flavors. The wedges are delicious served as a side dish with most meat, poultry, or fish kabobs, or just enjoyed on their own with lemon wedges and creamy yogurt.

Preheat the oven to 400°F.

Place the sweet potatoes in an ovenproof dish with the ginger and garlic. Pour in the olive oil, toss well, to coat the sweet potatoes and place them in the preheated oven for about 40 minutes, until the sweet potato is tender and slightly caramelized. Season to taste.

Serve the potato wedges as an accompaniment to kabobs or enjoy them on their own with lemon wedges for squeezing and a generous dollop of yogurt.

Index

almonds: spicy chicken kabobs with ground almonds 30

beef: fiery beef satay in peanut sauce 14
spicy beef and coconut kofta kabobs 18
bell peppers: shrimp and scallop kabobs with walnut sauce 46
summer vegetable kabobs with homemade pesto sauce 49
bulgur with ghee 58

cauliflower fritter satay with cilantro and coconut chutney 57
char-grilled tamarind shrimp 37
chermoula, monkfish kabobs with 41
chicken: chicken tandoori kabobs 26
gingery chicken tikka kabobs with minted yogurt 29
harissa chicken kabobs with oranges and preserved lemon 22
lemon chicken kabobs wrapped in eggplant 25
spicy chicken kabobs with ground almonds 30
chickpeas: hot hummus 9
cilantro and coconut chutney 57
couscous, buttery 58
cumin-flavored lamb kabobs with hot hummus 9
curried pork satay with pineapple sauce 13
duck satay with grilled pineapple and plum sauce 33

eggplants: lemon chicken kabobs wrapped in eggplant 25
pan-grilled eggplant with honey and spices 54
summer vegetable kabobs with homemade pesto sauce 49

fiery beef satay in peanut sauce 14
fish: vine-wrapped fish kabobs with tangy herb sauce 34
fritters: cauliflower fritter satay with cilantro and coconut chutney 57

garlic: roasted sweet potato with garlic and ginger 62
ginger: gingery chicken tikka kabobs with minted yogurt 29
roasted sweet potato with

garlic and ginger 62
simple noodles with ginger and chile 61

harissa chicken kabobs with oranges and preserved lemon 22
herbs: vine-wrapped fish kabobs with tangy herb sauce 34
honey: pan-grilled eggplant with honey and spices 54
hummus, hot 9

kofta kabobs: pork kofta kabobs with sweet and sour sauce 17
spicy beef and coconut kofta kabobs

lamb: cumin-flavored lamb kabobs with hot hummus 9
lamb and porcini kabobs with sage and Parmesan 21
lamb shish kabob with yogurt and flatbread 10
lemon chicken kabobs wrapped in eggplant 25

monkfish kabobs with chermoula 41
mushrooms: lamb and porcini kabobs with sage and Parmesan 21
noodles with ginger and chile 61

oranges: harissa chicken kabobs with oranges and preserved lemon 22
swordfish kabobs with oranges and sumac 38

peanut sauce, fiery beef satay in 14
peri-peri shrimp satay 45
pesto: summer vegetable kabobs with homemade pesto sauce 49
pilaf, rice 61
pineapple: curried pork satay with pineapple sauce 13
duck satay with grilled pineapple and plum sauce 33
plum sauce, duck satay with grilled pineapple and 33
pork: curried pork satay with pineapple sauce 13
pork kofta kabobs with sweet and sour sauce 17
pumpkin: roasted pumpkin wedges with lime and spices 53

sardines, stuffed char-grilled 42
satay: cauliflower fritter satay with cilantro and coconut chutney 57
curried pork satay with pineapple sauce 13
duck satay with grilled pineapple and plum sauce 33
fiery beef satay in peanut sauce 14
peri-peri shrimp satay 45
spicy tofu satay with soy dipping sauce 50
scallops: shrimp and scallop kabobs with walnut sauce 46
shrimp: char-grilled tamarind shrimp 37
peri-peri shrimp satay 45
shrimp and scallop kabobs with walnut sauce 46
soy dipping sauce 50
spicy beef and coconut kofta kabobs 18
spicy chicken kabobs with ground almonds 30
spicy tofu satay with soy dipping sauce 50
summer vegetable kabobs with homemade pesto sauce 49
sweet and sour sauce, pork kofta kabobs with 17
sweet potatoes: roasted sweet potato with garlic and ginger 62
swordfish kabobs with oranges and sumac 38

tamarind shrimp, char-grilled 37
tofu: spicy tofu satay with soy dipping sauce 50
tomatoes: lamb shish kabob with yogurt and flatbread 10
monkfish kabobs with chermoula 41
summer vegetable kabobs with homemade pesto sauce 49

vine-wrapped fish kabobs with tangy herb sauce 34
walnut sauce, shrimp and scallop kabobs with 46

yogurt: gingery chicken tikka kabobs with minted yogurt 29
lamb shish kabob with yogurt and flatbread 10
zucchini: summer vegetable kabobs with homemade pesto sauce 49

Conversion chart

Volume equivalents:

American	Metric	Imperial
6 tbsp butter	85 g	3 oz.
7 tbsp butter	100 g	3½ oz.
1 stick butter	115 g	4 oz.
1 teaspoon	5 ml	
1 tablespoon	15 ml	
¼ cup	60 ml	2 fl.oz.
⅓ cup	75 ml	2½ fl.oz.
½ cup	125 ml	4 fl.oz.
⅔ cup	150 ml	5 fl.oz. (¼ pint)
¾ cup	175 ml	6 fl.oz.
1 cup	250 ml	8 fl.oz.

Oven temperatures:

120°C/130°C	(250˚F)	Gas ½
140°C	(275°F)	Gas 1
150°C	(300°F)	Gas 2
160°C/170°C	(325°F)	Gas 3
180°C	(350°F)	Gas 4
190°C	(375°F)	Gas 5
200°C	(400°F)	Gas 6
220°C	(425°F)	Gas 7

Weight equivalents:

Imperial	Metric
1 oz.	30 g
2 oz.	55 g
3 oz.	85 g
3½ oz.	100 g
4 oz.	115 g
5 oz.	140 g
6 oz.	175 g
8 oz. (½ lb.)	225 g
9 oz.	250 g
10 oz.	280 g
11½ oz.	325 g
12 oz.	350 g
13 oz.	375 g
14 oz.	400 g
15 oz.	425 g
16 oz. (1 lb.)	450 g

Measurements:

Inches	Cm
¼ inch	0.5 cm
½ inch	1 cm
¾ inch	1.5 cm
1 inch	2.5 cm
2 inches	5 cm
3 inches	7 cm
4 inches	10 cm
5 inches	12 cm
6 inches	15 cm
7 inches	18 cm
8 inches	20 cm
9 inches	23 cm
10 inches	25 cm
11 inches	28 cm
12 inches	30 cm